Lewis Jones

FOCUS ON

GREAT BRITAIN

Hamish Hamilton · London

The author and publishers would like to thank the following
for permission to reproduce photographs: Barnaby's Picture
Library, cover; British Tourist Authority 16, 25 (left), 27
(right), 31; Chris Fairclough 24 (left), 26 (left); Steve Finnegan
11 (top); Susan Griggs Agency 3, 6 (right), 7, 8 (left), 9, 12
(right), 14 (right), 17 (left and right), 19 (left), 21 (right), 25
(right); Robert Harding Associates 10, 29 (right); John Hillelson
11 (bottom), 13, 14 (left), 15, 19 (right), 26 (right), 27 (left), 28
(right); Anwar Hussein 23, 30; Tony Stone Photolibrary 1, 6
(left), 8 (right), 12 (left), 18, 20, 21 (left), 22, 24 (right), 28 (left),
29 (left).

Design by Andrew Shoolbred

Map by Tony Garrett

Illustrations by Louis Mackay, Linda Rogers Associates

First published in Great Britain 1985 by
Hamish Hamilton Children's Books
Garden House, 57–59 Long Acre, London, WC2E 9JZ
Copyright © 1985 by Lewis Jones

British Library Cataloguing in Publication Data
Jones, Lewis
Focus on Great Britain.—(Focus on)
1. Great Britain—Social life and customs—
1945–   — Juvenile literature
I. Title
941.085'8   DA588
ISBN 0-241-11481-0

Printed in Italy by
New Interlitho S.p.A.

Cover: Punch and Judy shows are a
traditional part of a British seaside holiday.
Sometimes, the puppets can be quite
frightening, although the stories always seem
to end happily.

Previous page: Snowdon, at 1085 metres, is
the highest mountain in Wales. The
spectacular mountain scenery of Snowdonia
makes this a popular area for tourists and
climbers.

Terraced houses, known as 'back-to- ▶
backs', used to be common all over Britain.
Here in Newcastle, many people still live in
back-to-backs. Because the houses have no
gardens, washing is hung out to dry in the
streets.

Contents

Introducing Great Britain

Great Britain is an island made up of three countries – Scotland in the north, Wales in the west, and England. It is part of the United Kingdom, which also includes the six counties of Northern Ireland and many small islands such as the Isle of Wight, the Isles of Scilly, Anglesey, and the Orkneys, Shetlands and Hebrides. Great Britain alone has an area of just over 229,000 square kilometres. This is about the same size as West Germany or New Zealand, or half the size of France.

Inside Great Britain, people can travel freely from one country to another. There is only a sign at the side of the road to say you have crossed the border. The Scots, Welsh and the English are all British and, with the inhabitants of Northern Ireland, are all governed by Parliament in London. When abroad, they have British passports, and their cars display GB stickers.

The people

Ever since the Romans first arrived in Great Britain in 55 BC, people from other countries have come and settled here. Some came in search of land or work; others to escape a difficult way of life at home. Many brought new ideas and skills.

Throughout this century, people have continued to settle in Great Britain, although in recent years even more have left to live abroad. In the 1950s, many Hungarians fled to Britain after Russia invaded their homeland; in the 1950s and 60s, people from India, Pakistan and the Caribbean came to fill job vacancies which existed at that time; and in the 1980s the boat people from Vietnam arrived.

The land

Although Great Britain is quite a small island, and has a population of over 54 million, visitors are often surprised to discover how uncrowded it feels. Outside the main towns and cities, many of the smaller towns and villages look much as they did a century or so ago. Often the people who live in them come from families who settled there generations ago. The countryside, too, remains largely unspoilt. Even those who travel only a short distance soon realise how quickly the scenery can change from rolling hills to bleak moorland, to lush farmland.

Outer Hebrides

North West Highlands

Inner Hebrides

Loch Ness

Shetland Islands
• Sullom Voe

• Flotta
Orkney Islands

Grampians
△ Ben Nevis
SCOTLAND
Perth •
Loch Lomond
R. Forth
Glasgow • R. Clyde **Edinburgh** •
R. Tweed

Southern Uplands

R. Tyne • Newcastle upon Tyne

R. Tees Teesside

Scafell Pike △
Lake District
Pennines
R. Swale
R. Derwent
Scarborough •

North Sea

Isle of Man

Blackpool • Bradford • Leeds • Hull •

Liverpool • Manchester Grimsby •

Anglesey Sheffield • ENGLAND

Caernarvon △ Snowdon
Snowdonia
Porthmadog • Blaenau Llangollen
Ffestiniog Nottingham •

Birmingham • Midlands Norwich •

WALES Rugby • East Anglia

R. Severn Northampton • Felixstowe •

Swansea • High St. Albans
Wycombe • **London**
Cardiff •
R. Thames
Bristol • Dover •

Salisbury • Southampton • Brighton •

Atlantic Ocean Axminster • Portsmouth •
Isle of Wight

Plymouth • Dartington • English Channel

Isles of Scilly

Irish Sea

0   50   100 miles
0   50   100 kms

N

A varied landscape

It is only about 1000 kilometres from the northernmost tip of Scotland to England's south coast. Yet Great Britain contains many different landscapes.

Highland areas

Most of the high ground is in the north and west. The highest mountains of all are in Scotland, and Ben Nevis (1343 metres) is the highest peak. The rocks that form the Scottish Highlands are some of the oldest in Britain. In bad weather they can look bleak and forbidding. Along the north-west coast, the sea has worn away the rocks to form deep inlets and lakes, known as lochs.

In Wales, the highest peak is Snowdon (1085 metres). This is part of Snowdonia in North Wales, an area of spectacular mountain scenery which attracts many climbers and tourists each summer. For the less active, a good way of seeing the mountains is to take a trip on the mountain railway from Blaenau-Ffestiniog to Porthmadog.

The highest mountain in England is Scafell Pike (978 metres) in the Lake District, Cumbria. Hikers and ramblers come here to walk among the hills and enjoy the open views. Other visitors come to see the places described in the poems of William Wordsworth, one of England's greatest poets. Wordsworth was born in Cumbria and wrote about his childhood home in a very long poem called *The Prelude*.

Loch Duich and the Kintail mountains in north-west Scotland.

A lonely farmhouse in the Cumbrian hills.

The Pennines, the 'backbone of England', are a chain of limestone mountains that run for 240 kilometres down the centre of the country. Like most other highland areas, the soil is thin and poor. Few things will grow, except heather, gorse and grass, and so the land is mainly used for grazing sheep.

Lowland areas

Low-lying areas are mostly found in south and east Britain. The flattest area of all is East Anglia. Unlike in hillier areas, the soil here is rich and fertile. Most of the land is used for growing potatoes and vegetables.

Many people spend their holidays in East Anglia. They usually go to a

The Norfolk Broads are a popular area for boating holidays.

network of lakes, rivers and canals called the Norfolk Broads. Long ago, this whole area was dry. But when the peat beneath the soil was dug up for fuel, the land level dropped and water flowed in. The Broads have been flooded ever since. Nowadays, visitors to the Broads can enjoy a wide range of activities, including sailing, rowing, water-skiing and fishing. Nature lovers can watch the huge variety of birds which flock to the reed beds.

Farmland

Hundreds of years ago, much of lowland Britain was covered with forest. Since then, most of the trees have been cut down for timber, and the only large stretches of woodland left are in northern England, on the Welsh border and in some parts of south-east England. But the Government is encouraging farmers to protect their woodlands and to replace any trees cut down with young saplings. Most of the new woodlands are planted with pine trees (conifers) instead of the slower growing broad-leaved trees native to England and Wales.

Elsewhere, most of the rest of the land is farmland. Much of it is pasture for cows and sheep, and visitors to Britain often admire the vivid green of the grass. This is mainly due to the fairly cool, even climate with plentiful rain all year round.

7

Farming

The picture below shows the kind of view you might see from an aeroplane over Britain. The fields are large and divided up by hedges, walls or fences. Each one is used to grow a single crop, so that at a distance the land looks like a giant chessboard with squares of different colours.

A colourful patchwork of fields in the Midlands.

Farm animals

Although fewer than three people in every hundred work in farming, British farmers produce nearly two-thirds of all Britain's food. More than half of all farms concentrate on dairy or beef cattle, or sheep. Most of the dairy herds are made up of Jersey, Guernsey or Ayrshire cows. They provide enough milk, butter and cheese for all

Dairy cows grazing in Devon.

Britain's needs. Most British cheeses are hard and crumbly; they are usually named after the place where they were first made. In the 1980s, Britain produced a new cheese called Lymeswold, the first for two hundred years.

The most popular cheeses

1 English Cheddar	5 Caerphilly
2 Cheshire	6 Wensleydale
3 Double Gloucester	7 Lancashire
4 Leicester	8 Stilton

Beef cattle are fattened on low-lying grasslands and in enclosures on arable farms. Their meat is used for food, and their skin to provide leather.

The majority of sheep are also raised for food. But their wool is also important. Fleeces from short-haired breeds are best for knitting yarns, while those from long-haired mountain breeds (like the Blackface sheep) are made into carpets and rough cloth.

Food from the ground

Britain's two main cereal crops are barley and wheat. They are grown in eastern and central southern England and eastern Scotland. Five-sixths of the barley is used for animal food. The rest is used to make beer and whisky. Many of the biggest breweries are in the Midlands. The best known whisky distilleries are in Scotland.

Two-thirds of Britain's wheat also goes to feed animals. Most of the rest is used to make flour. Much of this flour is made into bread and cakes. British people are very fond of heavy fruit cakes, pies, biscuits and tea breads.

Vegetables and fruit

Britain also grows much of its own vegetables and fruit. The most important crop of all is potatoes. There are lots of different varieties, which are grown mostly in central and eastern England. The most famous is the King Edward potato.

Raspberry picking in Perthshire.

Some fruits, such as blackberries and bilberries, grow wild in hedgerows and on moors. Perthshire, in Scotland, is famous for its raspberries. In the autumn, you can sometimes see people picking them. But most fruits are specially grown in 'nurseries' in southern England. Kent is famous for its apple orchards, and is sometimes called the 'garden of England'. It grows two main kinds of apples: cooking apples (such as Bramley seedlings) and eating apples (like Cox's Orange Pippins). Some apples are made into cider.

9

Food

Until recently, British food was thought to be dull and badly cooked. This was partly because the British people have always liked plain, filling food, and partly because they are often unwilling to try anything new. But now more people are taking an interest in foreign foods and wines. As a result, they are also demanding a higher standard of cooking for traditional British dishes.

The English breakfast

One meal that has always had many admirers is the old-fashioned English breakfast. This usually consists of bacon and eggs and sometimes sausages, kidneys and tomatoes as well! It is rounded off with toast, butter and marmalade (a kind of bitter jam made from Seville oranges). Few people nowadays eat this kind of breakfast every day. Instead, they probably make do with a bowl of cereal and a cup of tea.

Scottish food

Scotland's best known food is haggis. This is eaten on Burns Night, the 25th January. (Robert Burns is Scotland's

Haggis and mashed potatoes

national poet.) Haggis is made from lamb's liver, sheep's heart, suet, oatmeal, onions and seasoning. The ingredients are all mixed together and then stuffed into a sheep's stomach and steamed. Haggis is usually served with 'bashed neeps' (mashed turnips).

Welsh food

Wales is particularly well known for its baking, and it still produces many different kinds of breads and pastries. One of the better known is 'bara brith', which means 'speckled bread' in Welsh. This is a dark fruity bread made with flour, yeast, brown sugar, butter, eggs, currants and raisins. Sliced and spread thickly with butter, it makes a delicious tea-time snack.

Another famous dish is Welsh rarebit. The Welsh call this dish 'caws pobi', which means 'baked cheese'. The recipe below tells you how to make it.

Ingredients
(to serve four)

25g butter, melted
1 level tsp English mustard
175g Cheddar cheese, finely grated
½ tsp Worcester sauce
2 tblsp milk
4 large slices bread, lightly toasted
on both sides

1 Mix butter with mustard, cheese, Worcester sauce and add milk.
2 Spread equal amounts fairly thickly on one side of each piece of toast.
3 Brown under a hot grill. (Ask an adult to do this for you.)

Eating out

Unlike the French or Italians, most British people only go to eat at a restaurant on a special occasion. Eating out can be very expensive. But during the last twenty years or so, cheaper, more informal restaurants have begun to appear. Nearly every town and village now has at least one Indian or Chinese restaurant, serving good quality inexpensive food. Other foods, such as pasta and pizzas (from Italy)

Breakfast in a London café.

and hamburgers (from America) are also popular.

Nearly all these new restaurants offer a take-away service. Customers order what they want, wait a few minutes, then take the food home to eat. The first take-away of all was the fish and chip shop. The original fish and chip shop opened over a hundred years ago, and others soon followed. Today, fish and chip shops use nearly half of all Britain's white fish and a tenth of Britain's potatoes.

A thriving 'take-away' in Polperro, Cornwall.

Power and industry

Britain has the largest natural sources of power of any country in the European community. In addition to relying on coal, oil, and gas, nuclear power has been produced for several decades. In 1956 the world's first large scale nuclear power station opened at Calder Hall (Cumbria), and in 1980 Britain became self-sufficient in energy.

Miners in Wales, one of Britain's major coal producing areas.

Coal

Traditionally, Britain has relied on coal to produce power. Britain's coal industry is still the largest in Western Europe. It is also one of the most advanced. However, the discovery of large supplies of oil in the North Sea has led to a decline in the importance of coal.

Oil

Oil was first brought ashore from the North Sea in 1975. Since then Britain has become the world's sixth largest oil producer. Burning oil is a lot cleaner than burning coal, but it is a more expensive way of producing power.

An offshore oil rig on a very calm day in the North Sea.

Nuclear power

Nuclear power stations – reactors – get their power from atoms of uranium. Some scientists say that these power stations are very clean and safe; others claim that they are dangerous.

Whoever is right, they already provide nearly a fifth of all Britain's electricity.

As well as researching into ways of improving the safety of power stations, scientists are trying to work out ways of harnessing power from the sun, the tide and waves. This requires a lot of inventiveness. Britain is a leader in the field of inventions. Some examples of famous 'firsts' are –

1589	Water closet (lavatory)	1900	Loudspeaker
		1913	Stainless steel
1689	Steam engine	1926	Television
1804	Locomotive	1937	Jet engine
1824	Cement	1941	Terylene
1826	Safety match	1955	Hovercraft
1837	Ship's propeller		
1839	Bicycle		
1846	Rubber tyre		
1853	Glider		
1883	Rayon		

Britain's inventiveness has often helped British industry.

The car industry

Britain was one of the first nations to manufacture cars. The car industry is centred in the Midlands. This is where the Metro, the Landrover and the Jaguar are made. Some cars are exported all over the world because

A modern car factory in the Midlands.

they are famous for their reliability. Over half the Rolls-Royce cars built since 1904 are still in use.

The chemical industry

The newly emerging chemical industry is one of Britain's most successful. As well as manufacturing and developing many essential drugs which help in the treatment of heart disease, arthritis, ulcers and cancer, Britain plays an important role in the production of man-made fibres.

Examples of things you might see in your home that were made in Britain are –

Carpets from Axminster
Shoes from Northampton
Knitwear from Scotland
Glass from Dartington
Knives and forks from Sheffield
Furniture from High Wycombe

All at sea

Great Britain is a long thin island – so thin that no place is farther than 120 kilometres from the sea. Until the 19th century, sea air and sea water were thought to cure all sorts of illnesses. It became fashionable for rich people to go to the seaside for their health. And later, towns like Scarborough on the east coast, and Brighton on the south, became popular places for a holiday. Nowadays, seaside towns attract many thousands of people every summer. The most popular of all is probably Blackpool on the north-west coast.

Brighton beach is a popular place for day-trippers on a hot summer's day.

Devon and Cornwall

For people who don't like big seaside towns like Blackpool, there are still many 'unspoiled' stretches of coastline. One of the most beautiful is around Devon and Cornwall in south-west England. Here the coastline is jagged

The jagged coastline around Cornwall, where 'wreckers' once lured ships onto the rocks.

and steep. Until the last century, many ships were wrecked on the rocks. People called 'wreckers' used to lure the ships onto the rocks with lamps. When the ship had sunk, they would steal cargo that washed ashore.

Nowadays, holidaymakers come here to enjoy the sandy beaches or, if they are fit, to walk along the coastal path. In recent years, Cornwall has become a popular place for surfing.

Fishing

The sea not only gives pleasure; it also provides food. Once, fishermen used to catch fish off nearly all Britain's coasts. But now most work in the North Sea, off north-east England and eastern Scotland. The biggest fishing port is Grimsby.

Most fishermen work on freezer trawlers, which can stay at sea for weeks at a time. They sail a long way from land, where waves can be over 30 metres high, and winds can reach speeds of over 200 kph. Here they trawl for white fish such as cod, haddock, plaice and skate.

After the fish have been caught, they are stored in huge freezer compartments below deck. Here, they will be frozen until they can be unloaded, sorted and washed. At big fishing ports like Grimsby and Hull, the fish are taken straight to nearby food factories to be made into fish fingers and other frozen foods.

London Dock is one of Britain's busiest container ports.

Ports

There are over 300 ports in Great Britain, although most of them are small harbours and do not handle cargo regularly. At most of the larger ports, such as London, Southampton and Felixstowe, much of the cargo is now transported in containers. These are huge steel boxes, specially designed to stack neatly on board ship. Enormous cranes are used for loading and unloading.

Ports which have not been able to adapt to containers have lost business. Some ports in northern England and Scotland have also suffered because two new ports have been built to handle oil from the North sea. These are at Flotta in Orkney and Sullom Voe in Shetland.

15

Going places

Roads

Most travelling in Britain is done by road. The first roads were built by the Romans, and were usually very straight. Some are still in use today. The oldest is called Watling Street, and runs from the City of London to St Albans in Hertfordshire.

More recently, motorways have been built to link major towns and important industrial areas. One of the busiest is the M6. This provides a direct route between Birmingham and the north-west.

Good fast roads are very important because nearly all goods are transported by road. Without motorways, there would be traffic jams and delays. Meat, fish, vegetables and flowers would go bad before they could be sold; and other goods, such as coal, would miss important delivery dates.

Long-distance lorries and cars use ring roads and bypasses to avoid going through towns they do not have to visit. This has two main advantages: journey-times are shorter; and town centres are less crowded, and so quieter and safer.

A straight Roman road stretching its way across Wheeldale moor in Yorkshire.

All roads are given a letter and a number. The letter shows what kind of road it is.

M Motorway

A Major route

B Minor route

R Ring road

A steam-powered train on the Bluebell Railway in Sussex.

An inter-city train at York, on its way from Scotland to London.

Railways

Great Britain has always been proud of its railways. In 1825, the world's first passenger steam train was opened in north-east England. This was the Stockton and Darlington Railway. Since then a fast network of trains has been developed, linking all major towns in Great Britain. However, many smaller, branch-line routes have been closed. So few people were using them that it became too costly to maintain them.

The railway network is run by British Rail, who have recently introduced two new trains – the HST (High Speed Train) and the APT (Advanced Passenger Train). Both can travel at a speed of 125 mph. The APT can also corner much faster than ordinary trains.

When the HST (usually known as the Inter-City) was introduced in 1976, it became the world's fastest diesel railway service. The journey-time between London and Edinburgh, for example, was cut by 38 minutes to under five hours. Since then, both the French and Japanese have developed trains which can travel even faster.

British Rail owns and runs most railway track throughout Britain. But there are also over forty small privately owned railways. These are run mostly for tourists and steam train enthusiasts. The smallest of all is the Romney, Hythe and Dymchurch Railway in Kent, south-east England. Other well known steam railways are the Ffestiniog Railway in Wales and the Bluebell Line in southern England.

Inside Wales

The Welsh people are very proud of their language and culture. In some remote parts of Wales, Welsh is the only language spoken. Elsewhere it is taught in schools and used on Welsh television programmes. Visitors to Wales will see road signs written in Welsh. If you ever go there, look out for a sign with the words, 'Croeso I Cymru'. This means 'Welcome to Wales'.

A separate country?

For hundreds of years Wales was a separate country from England. There were many battles along the border, and the English built castles to try and subdue their neighbours. You can still see some of them today. It was not until 1283 that the Welsh were finally conquered by Edward I of England.

In 1284, King Edward travelled to Caernarvon in north Wales. Here his son was born. At a special ceremony a few days later the King showed the baby prince to the crowd, saying 'Here is your King'. Ever since, the oldest son of the reigning king or queen has become Prince of Wales.

But there are still some Welsh people today who feel that Wales should be completely free from England. This group of people call themselves 'Plaid Cymru', which means 'Party of Wales'. Their headquarters are in Cardiff, the Welsh capital.

Caernarvon castle, where the first Prince of Wales was born in 1284. Prince Charles was crowned Prince of Wales here in 1969.

A typical mining village in the Rhondda
England, Wales and Scotland each
pit head itself.

Welsh mining villages

Most people in Wales live in the south.
This is where the coal fields are. Coal-
mining is Wales's most important
industry. The coal earns money for
Wales and the mining provides jobs for
the people.

In recent years, some of the pits
have been closed because the cost of
mining has become so great. Now many
people are afraid the whole industry
will collapse. Despite Government
schemes to attract new industries to
Wales, there are still only a few
alternatives to becoming a miner.

Welsh customs

People in mining villages are not only
worried about losing their jobs. They
are also afraid that Welsh customs and
traditions may disappear. One of the
best known is the 'eisteddfod' (this is a
Welsh word meaning 'sitting'). An
eisteddfod is a competition held in
many towns each year to find the best
singers and poets in the area. The
biggest international eisteddfod takes
place in Llangollen in north Wales.

People joining in an eisteddfod wear the
costume once worn by their Celtic ancestors.

England, Wales and Scotland each
have their own patron saint and
national emblem.

Flag	Saint	Emblem
✚	St George 23rd April	
🐉	St David 1st March	
✕	St Andrew 30th November	

Inside Scotland

The Romans did not conquer Scotland. Being such a long way from home, they found it impossible to quell the fierce northerners called the Picts. The language spoken by the Picts was Gaelic, and Gaelic words are still in use today – for example, clan, loch and glen. But Gaelic as a language is only spoken by a few people in the Highlands and Islands.

Scotland and England were joined fairly peacefully. Almost three hundred years ago, England's Queen Elizabeth 1st died, leaving no children to inherit the throne. Her nearest relative was King James 6th of Scotland, who then became King James 1st of England too. This joining of the two countries produced a flag that brought together the cross of Saint George (England) and the cross of Saint Andrew (Scotland). When the Irish cross of Saint Patrick was added later, all three combined to form the Union flag – the official flag of the United Kingdom.

Some Scottish people want Scotland to be entirely independent of the United Kingdom. Many of them are represented by the Scottish National Party. However, the SNP have only won a few seats in Parliament.

Clans

Many Scots (and people of Scottish descent all over the world) can claim to belong to a family group called a clan. Each clan has one or more distinctive tartans. A tartan is a woollen cloth woven in a pattern of coloured squares called a check. The Scottish kilt, a kind of pleated skirt, is normally made out of tartan.

The spectacular tartans of the Shotts and Dykehead Caledonian Pipe Band.

A panoramic view of Edinburgh, home of the famous international festival.

Cities

Edinburgh is the capital city and centre of Scotland's banking and legal systems. Scots law is quite different from English law.

For three weeks each summer, Edinburgh hosts a large festival which attracts thousands of artists and visitors from all over the world. One of the most popular events is the Edinburgh tattoo. This is a performance of music, dancing and marching by military bands and Highland dancers. The tattoo takes place beneath floodlights in front of Edinburgh castle. Tiers of seats are specially built to accommodate all the spectators.

Glasgow is Scotland's largest city. At one time, it was famous for heavy industry, and ship-building in particular. But then the demand for ships dropped and Glasgow had a difficult few years. Today, Glasgow is encouraging light industry and small businesses to come to the city.

Scotland's third largest city is Aberdeen in the north-east. In recent years, Aberdeen has become the centre of Scotland's part in the North Sea oil industry. It has become a prosperous town, although it is also a very expensive place to live.

Whisky

Scottish whisky, or 'Scotch', has been made in Scotland for hundreds of years, and is still an important product. The main ingredients are barley and water. The softness of Scottish water is supposed to give the whisky its special smooth flavour.

Whisky is Scotland's national drink, although much of it is exported. It is traditionally drunk on Hogmanay (New Year's Eve) and on Burns Night.

Distilling whisky in Islay, part of the Inner Hebrides.

Parliament

Great Britain has had kings and queens for over a thousand years. For more than half of that time, they ruled the country personally, with only a few advisors to help them. But gradually things became too difficult for one person to handle, and the first Parliament came into being.

The House of Commons

Today, Parliament is made up of two 'Houses' – the House of Commons and the House of Lords. The Commons has 650 'seats'. These are occupied by Members of Parliament (MPs) who each represent one area of the United Kingdom. All seats must be won in an

The Houses of Parliament towering above the River Thames. In the background is the clock tower which contains the famous bell, Big Ben.

election. Anyone over the age of eighteen, unless a life peer, in prison or mentally unfit, is allowed to vote.

Most people vote for someone who belongs to one of the three main 'parties' – the Conservatives, the Labour party, or the Social Democrats and Liberal party Alliance. A few vote for local parties such as Plaid Cymru or the Scottish National Party. The party which wins the greatest number of seats forms the Government. Its leader becomes Prime Minister.

The House of Lords

One of Parliament's main jobs is to make laws. Each new law must first be discussed by the House of Commons. MPs there talk and argue about it in three main 'readings' until they are satisfied it is correct. It is then passed to the House of Lords. Here a few more changes may be suggested, until the

A packed House of Lords watches the Queen opening Parliament.

law is finally 'passed'. The Queen gives the Royal Assent by signing the law, and from then on it must be obeyed.

Unlike in the Commons, members of the Lords are not elected. They either inherit their seat, or are given one because of their importance in the Church or Law. Some new members are created each year in the New Year, or Queen's Birthday Honours Lists.

Being an MP

Parliament is officially opened by the Queen in the autumn. She and other members of the royal family travel in state from Buckingham House to Westminster. There she reads a speech written by the Prime Minister, describing the Government's plans for the next year. She then gives her permission for Parliament to proceed.

Parliament sometimes has so much business to get through that MPs have to stay up all night. To show they are still 'sitting' a light is kept burning in the clock tower. This tower houses Big Ben, the bell whose chimes can be heard on the radio all over the world.

MPs do not always attend every session, so there is a complicated system of bells to warn them if they are wanted for a vote. If it is essential for MPs to be present, they are given a 'three-line whip'. This means they must go to Westminster to vote, even if they have to come back from holiday to do so!

London

London is the capital city of England, and the centre of government for the whole of Great Britain. It has been Britain's first city since the Romans decided it would make a good port. Modern London is the twenty-sixth largest city in the world, with over nine million inhabitants.

The City of London

The City of London is a small area of only two to three square kilometres, on the site of the original Roman settlement. It is London's business centre and one of the richest spots in the world. Many of the big banks have their head offices here, and the Bank of England has strongrooms below ground to store its gold.

During the week, the City streets are crowded with bankers, stockbrokers and office-workers. But in the evenings and at weekends, they are empty and quiet.

The 'sights'

Most tourists visit London to see sights such as the Tower of London, Buckingham Palace, the Houses of Parliament and St Paul's Cathedral.

St Paul's Cathedral.

A Beefeater at the Tower of London.

The Changing of the Guard at Buckingham Palace.

The Tower of London is an old castle near the River Thames. It was built by William I shortly after he invaded England in 1066. From then on it was often used as a prison, and many famous people were kept there. Some of them were beheaded on Tower Green. Nowadays, the Tower is a museum for the Crown Jewels. It is patrolled by wardens nicknamed Beefeaters. The design of their red and yellow costume is over 300 years old.

The 'tube'

One of the best ways of getting around is by using the underground railway, or 'tube'. With over 400 kilometres of track and 268 stations, the tube is the largest underground in the world.

During rush hours, so many people squash into the carriages that it can be difficult to get off at the right station.

The River Thames

Running through the centre of London is the River Thames. At one time, the river was so dirty that no fish could live in the water. But now it is much cleaner and even quite unlikely fish, such as salmon, can be found in it.

At the mouth of the Thames is the Port of London. This is one of Britain's largest ports, handling over 35 million tonnes of cargo a year. If a large ocean-going ship wants to sail up the Thames, Tower Bridge opens to let it through.

Further upstream, at Woolwich Reach, is the Thames flood barrier. It was opened by the Queen in 1984. This is a kind of enormous gate which can be raised to block dangerous surges of sea water. When the water level has dropped, the gate is lowered onto the river bed.

The Thames flood barrier was opened by the Queen in 1984.

At home

About two hundred years ago, four out of every five people lived in the country. Then during the nineteenth century people began to drift to the towns in search of work in the newly built factories. Today, nearly everyone lives in a town or city.

Housing

Older towns and cities contain houses of many different ages and styles. Some can be several hundred years old, although nearly half have been built during the last forty years.

Semi-detached houses near London.

Terraced houses are common all over Britain. These are houses which are built in a row, so that each house is joined by another on either side. They are cheaper to build than semi-detached houses (which are joined on one side only) or detached houses. Although nearly all have their own garden, they do not have a garage. So many people own a car now that car-parking has become a big problem.

Nearly three-quarters of all people living in Britain live in houses. The rest live in flats. During the 1950s and 60s, huge blocks of flats, called tower blocks, were built. But few people liked living so far above ground. Mothers with young children complained that there was nowhere for their children to play. Today no tower

Modern flats in Surrey Docks.

blocks are being built. Instead, people choose to live in 'low rise' blocks of flats, or in large old houses which have been divided up and modernised.

New towns

Since the 1940s, thirty-two 'new towns' have been built. They were planned by the Government to ease housing and employment problems in some of the older towns. The town of Washington, near Newcastle, was carefully planned to hold 50,000 people. It was divided into separate districts called 'villages'. Each village has its own houses, shops, schools and pubs. The factories are built away from the houses, but close enough for people to be able to walk to work.

Market towns

Some of the prettiest towns in Britain are the old market towns. Before the big industrial towns grew up, people used to come to towns like Uttoxeter in Staffordshire to buy or sell goods, and to catch up on local gossip.

The pretty market town of Uttoxeter.

Gardening is a favourite British pastime.

At home

In Britain, it is nearly everyone's ambition to buy his or her own home. To do this, people usually have to borrow a lot of money from a building society or bank. They pay back the loan over a period of twenty-five years.

Most British people are very proud of their house and garden. They spend a lot of free time on DIY (Do-It-Yourself) improvements to their houses, and on gardening. Even if their garden is quite small, they take endless time and trouble looking after their lawn, flower-beds and vegetable plots.

27

Sports and pastimes

Football

The British invented many of the sports and pastimes which are now played all over the world. The most popular of them all is probably football. The rules for association football were developed in England during the nineteenth century. Now it is controlled by separate football associations in England, Wales, and Scotland. There are football teams in almost every part of Britain, and they play against one another in league matches. The football season lasts from August until May. During this time, about nineteen million people go to football league matches in England alone.

Rugby football

Rugby football takes its name from Rugby school, in Warwickshire, where it was first played in 1823. The game was invented by accident when one of the boys decided to pick up the ball and run with it instead of kicking it. Rugby now has a strict set of rules, and international matches between England, Scotland, Wales, Ireland and France are played each year. The Welsh are considered to be especially talented players.

Football fans turn out in force to support their teams.

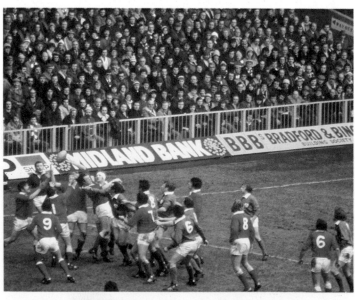

Welsh rugby players (in red) in action.

John McEnroe on the famous centre court at Wimbledon.

Annual events

Every June television sets all over the world show hours of play from one of the world's most famous tennis tournaments. This takes place at Wimbledon in south London. The championship has been running since 1877. An English player, Virginia Wade, won the women's singles title in the centenary year. However, a British man hasn't won a singles title since Fred Perry in 1936.

In summer and autumn every year, Highland games are held in Scotland. The most famous take place in August at Braemar. The games are largely a male affair, and every man must wear a kilt. At the games, competitors may test their strength by trying to toss the caber. (A caber is the trunk of a young tree.) The tosser rests it on his shoulder, runs forward, and hurls it into the air. A champion may hurl it more than twelve metres. But for sixty years until 1951, no one succeeded in tossing the Braemar caber at all. It is almost six metres long and weighs fifty-four kilograms.

Pastimes

The British love competing, even against fish. Sitting on a river bank with a fishing rod is one of their favourite leisure-time activities.

The most popular pastime of all is watching television. But even then, the programmes which attract the most viewers involve competition – whether this is between players at a snooker table, or farmers trying to win the sheepdog trials. One British family in every four has a video cassette recorder, a higher percentage than in any other country in the world.

Peace and solitude on the riverside.

Great Britain and the world

The Empire

About four hundred years ago, British explorers first set sail in search of unknown lands. They began a long tradition of settling down in faraway places, and some of these places became known as British colonies. Britain began to trade with them, and in time British people could be found in many different parts of the world — for example, Canada, Australia, New Zealand, Africa, Singapore, Hong Kong, and the Far East. This network of British colonies became the Empire, with the British king or queen at its head.

The Commonwealth

During the 20th century, more and more colonies decided to look after their own affairs and become independent. These countries have become equal partners with Britain, and make up what is known as the Commonwealth.

Today, there are forty-four Commonwealth countries. They are scattered around the world, and include places as far apart as Bangladesh, Malaysia, Jamaica, Cyprus,

The Queen greeting children on a Commonwealth tour of New Zealand.

Fiji and Papua New Guinea. The people who live in these countries are of different races, with different histories, different customs, and different religions. But even today, there are still strong links between them, and the Queen is still called the Head of the Commonwealth.

England and Australia battling for the 'Ashes' during the centenary test series in 1980.

Member nations also keep in touch with each other. The leaders have a formal meeting every two years to talk about Commonwealth affairs, and sports teams meet informally from time to time to play against each other. They take turns to visit each other's country as there are no Commonwealth headquarters.

The Common Market

Throughout her long history, Britain has fought many wars against European countries. But nowadays serious disagreements are less likely because several European countries have joined together to form the Common Market. This was set up shortly after the Second World War to try and prevent another such war ever happening again. It was also designed to allow people and goods to travel more easily between member countries. Great Britain joined the Common Market in 1973.

Common Market rules have changed Britain's trading pattern with the Commonwealth. Before 1973, most of Britain's imported food came from Commonwealth countries. Trading agreements meant that such food cost Britain less than it would from elsewhere. And the exporting countries had a secure market for their goods. Now Britain has to pay the full Market price for all her food.

But despite some disadvantages, most British people are glad to be part of Europe, and also to be a member of the Commonwealth. No other country in the world has such a network of friendly contacts.

Index and summary

Area:	229,979 square kilometres
Population:	54 million
Capital:	London
Main towns:	Birmingham, Glasgow, Leeds, Liverpool, Sheffield, Manchester, Edinburgh
Main exports:	Machinery, transport equipment, textiles, chemicals
Main imports:	Machinery, metals, transport equipment, paper, chemicals
Main crops:	Barley, wheat
Highest point:	Ben Nevis, in Scotland, 1343 metres
Longest river:	the Severn
Official language:	English
Currency:	100 pence to the £1
National airline:	British Airways